We Have Seen The Enemy
and They Are Odd

Christopher Gray

Sunbow Press

TORONTO

Copyright © 2013 by Christopher Gray
Published by Sunbow Press
Address inquiries to: sunbow.press@gmail.com

ISBN 978-0-9868364-7-3

Library and Archives Canada Cataloguing in Publication

Gray, Christopher, [date]
    We have seen the enemy and they are odd / Christopher Gray.

Issued also in electronic format.
ISBN 978-0-9868364-7-3 (pbk.)

        I. Title.

PS8613.R3875W44 2013   C813'.6   C2013-902441-7

"The only thing worse than being witty is **not** *being witty"*
– Monty Python

– 1 –

Within hours the comet had been catalogued by every civilian and military organization. Over the next two weeks news services gave periodic updates as the comet got closer to Earth and became visible first to small telescopes, then if the nights were clear to binoculars, then to the naked eye. The news reports also stated there was no danger of a collision with Earth.

At the Pentagon, Colonel Ford was in charge of the team tracking the comet for the US government. His aide, Lieutenant Gibson, in direct hourly communication with the astronomy team, had asked for an urgent meeting. The Colonel didn't like meetings, and he liked urgent ones even less.

"Lieutenant Gibson, your email said this Football Comet…"

"Comet Rugby-Jones sir. The discoverer was named Jones and it is shaped like a football, or rather a rugby ball, since the naming administration didn't want to confuse European observers, they—"

"Whatever. You said it was showing some anomalies. Just what the hell do you mean by that?"

"Well sir, it seems to be changing course. Slightly."

The colonel glared. He didn't want to repeat himself. The lieutenant cleared his throat.

"What I mean colonel is that Rugby-Jones is, uh, following a curved trajectory that will take it very close to the Earth. Dangerously close in fact, although there is still very little chance of a collision. It's due to arrive in two days."

"How is that possible? Was there an error in the initial course calculation?"

"No sir. Well, maybe. We need to do some checking."

Colonel Ford drummed his desk with his fingers.

"Well, be sure to tell us when you recheck the calculations. I believe the President would like to know just how close this Comet Rugby-Football will come, and if there is a danger it will smash into us! Don't you agree?"

"Comet Rugby-Jones sir."

"Dismissed!"

"Thank you sir."

– 2 –

Two days later the Lieutenant rushed into Colonel Ford's office.

"Sir, the comet is breaking up! But that's not the worst part. It appears to have broken into five equal parts, and they've formed a ring."

The Colonel was on the phone to his wife. He cupped the receiver.

"Jones-Football is breaking up?"

"Rugby-Jones sir."

"I'll call you back sweetheart," he said, as he placed the phone on its cradle. Gibson was pacing nervously.

"Calm down Lieutenant! What do you mean 'breaking up?'"

Gibson continued to pace back and forth in front of the Colonel's desk.

"I mean sir that the five pieces appear to be under intelligent control. They are in formation, changing course, headed this way."

The Colonel thought for a moment then picked up the phone.

"I'll call the Chief of Staff. We need to meet in the Control Room conference area. Get yourself back down there and find out specifically when these things are going to hit us. Move!"

Gibson exited double-time as Colonel Ford dialed the White House.

– 3 –

Twenty minutes later the President and his staff arrived in the Control Room at the Pentagon. A Vice Admiral of the Pacific Fleet, Major Scott of the Air Force, their aides, and a senior director from each of the FBI and Homeland Security were already present. The crowded room was medium-sized with a rectangular conference table in front of a large window overlooking a much larger room that resembled NASA's Mission Control. They could see about a dozen engineers at their workstations, and three large monitors on the far wall that could display satellite images, maps, television broadcasts, and virtually any other information. As the group sat down at the conference table Colonel Ford explained the situation.

"There are five ships in all, and they are attaining orbit above us as we speak."

"Ships?!?" the President said. "An hour ago this thing was just a comet."

"Yes sir, but in the last half hour what we thought was a comet separated into five equal pieces, each of which appears to be under independent control. They are maneuvering into high Earth orbit now."

There was a static sound coming from the large monitor speakers, and the screens flickered. Everyone in the room froze, staring at the screens.

"Message coming through on the . . . on the . . . no wait. It's two frequencies sir. A wireless telephony frequency and an HDTV frequency," a communications specialist called to the unit commander.

"A what?"

"Wireless . . . band sir. Uh . . . I've captured an LTE frequency sir and it's powerful," the comm specialist paused, frowning and staring at his screen. A pause, then, "Confirmed sir! And reports are flooding in from monitoring stations. The alien transmission momentarily overloaded the network, cutting off thousands of other calls."

"Display so we can see it, specialist" the unit commander ordered.

Everyone turned slightly to look at a large, central display. After a few seconds the message appeared:

Pepl of Earth. Prepare 2 B conkrd

The President and the Colonel looked at each other, then back to the screen.

"Another message sir," the comm specialist called.

"Don't keep us waiting specialist, put it up."

The message appeared:

U R no match 4 us. Lay down or we will Rul and waste ur world

The President said, "What the hell is this? A joke? Has some hacker tapped into our system?"

The Colonel waved Gibson over.

"Lieutenant! Find out if our system has been breached. I want to know where that message is really coming from!"

Gibson ran down the stairs and talked with the chief

engineer at the lead workstation. He looked back up at the conference room. He could be heard over the room's intercom.

"Sir, the team has been running intensive intrusion monitoring. Our network is 100% secure. This message came from space, from one of those orbiting ships. We can see the ship on the large monitor."

A flickering white shape appeared on a monitor. It was too fuzzy to make out clearly, but it was rugby-ball shaped. Inside the conference room the group looked back to the President.

"I don't understand this. If it weren't for those orbiting ships, I would think this was a joke. Who in hell sends idiotic messages like that. And why the threats? Is this how you contact a new race, by threatening them?"

Gibson had made his way back into the observation area.

"Sir, I have a theory. If the aliens were studying us for a period before arriving, and had access to email or phone text transmissions, they may believe this is the preferred way to communicate."

Colonel Ford huffed. "Terrific. The aliens are learning our language from lazy texters."

"Yes sir," Gibson said. "Nevertheless, the content of the message indicates a threat."

The President looked to one of his advisors. "I can't believe I'm actually saying this. Go to high alert," he said.

The advisor picked up the phone to carry out the order. An engineer at a workstation below gestured to Lieutenant Gibson, holding up a clipboard with a number on it. Gibson turned to the President.

"Sir, the engineers have the frequency on which the aliens transmitted. We can send a message to them if required."

The President thought for a moment. He took out his pen and began writing on a note pad.

"Normally we would strike a committee to compose a message, but this can't wait. Send the following message to the alien ship immediately."

He handed the paper to Colonel Ford, who upon reading it nodded and handed it off to Gibson, who took it down to the engineer. After a moment the outgoing message appeared on the view screen:

To unidentified ships: we wish to enter into peaceful dialog, but be advised we are capable of defending ourselves if necessary.

Fifteen seconds later there was a reply:

You are weak. You will be enslaved. You will cower in terror at our might.

The President looked grim. "That's their answer?" he asked, incredulous. "They sound like…" he paused, trying to find the right word. "They sound like… morons."

"At least their grammar has improved," said Colonel Ford.

– 4 –

The alien's transmission was not only seen at the Pentagon, but on every television on Earth. By now most people were aware that the comet was actually some sort of extraterrestrial craft and various news leaks had verified that several ships were in orbit. The messages were transmitted in English but once translated locally they caused worldwide panic.

The U.S. and dozens of other countries beamed more inquiries at the alien ships. There was no direct response or acknowledgement. After another hour had passed, the aliens broadcast more messages:

Watch in horror as our superior technology pulverizes your buildings!

Experience sadness as your military forces are defeated and your soldiers flee!

Be reduced to shame as your educated elites bow to us as slaves!

News headlines erupted everywhere with *They Mean To Destroy Us* and similar doomsday sentiments. Work stoppages occurred spontaneously. In some cities citizens rioted, but these were being quickly broken up almost as fast as they occurred as local police forces in hundreds of cities around the world were being beefed up by military personnel. People were urged to calm down and wait for more information about the aliens while governments invoked curfews. Some cities evacuated their citizens, while others allowed them to stay put.

Over the next week civil order returned but people continually demanded that their governments do something. Some outspoken individuals preached that the world should welcome the aliens as overlords. Church attendance went through the roof as many people feared this was the end of the world, or that they would be put under brutal rule by a superior race.

After a few days of silence from the aliens people went back to work, though they were still on edge. Even in areas without a curfew, nobody travelled unless necessary, preferring to stay near home with their loved ones.

There were continuous meetings in the Control Room. All five of the alien ships were in synchronous orbit, maintaining a position over each continent on Earth. The President was going over options with his advisors and Colonel Ford.

"Two weeks since the first messages. And nothing since. What is the latest intelligence on the ships? Can we defeat them Dr. Himmler?" the colonel asked, turning to face a man dressed in tweeds.

"Himmler?" the President whispered to his aide. "Any relation to…?"

"I think he's a nephew or something. Doesn't like to talk about it," the aide whispered back.

Dr. Henrik Himmler from MIT was lead analyst. He glanced down at a binder in front of him. He cleared his throat.

"Ve zdill cannot ackvire mooch uf a readink of zos szhips. Infraret is a leetl bedder, und gives uz ze approxzimatt zize uf eaj spazekraft at fife hundred meeders by sree hundred meeders."

"I don't understand a word he just said," the President whispered to his aide.

"Big enough to contain thousands of troops and their weapons," said Major Scott. "I've been working closely with Dr. Himmler."

"Ah," the President interjected. "Wait. What? You're thinking they mean to invade us? How effective will our defenses be?"

"Az menjhunned in ze Joint Chief's inizial report, ve haf mobilized our forzes, but vill not haf a broper defenzif blan undil zuj dime ass ve know more about ze aliens," Himmler stated, apparently looking calmly at a point on the far wall. "Zo far we do not know if zey blan to addack uz from orbit or lant an invasion forze. As ber your order, all uf our azzets are on high alert, und rezerfs haf been galled in. Zame mit our allies and even zoze states hozdile to ze Vest."

"I don't understand a damn word," the president whispered to his aide."

"If they attack from orbit will our ICBMs reach them?" one of the intelligence staff asked.

"Absolutely not," said Ford. "ICBMs are not designed for escape velocity. They follow a parabolic course to Earth-bound targets. We have some anti-satellite missiles that can attain low orbit but the aliens are too far out."

"And anyway, those missiles don't carry more than a few

pounds of explosive, since they are only designed to take out a typical small satellite," added Gibson.

The president drummed his fingers on the desk.

"So the next move is theirs."

At that moment an alarm went off in the Control Room. An engineer at a workstation below shouted, "Another message coming in!"

The large monitor screen went blank, then some text appeared.

We are launching the great invasion. We will smash your cities and enslave you!

The President slammed his fist on the table. "Launch all fighters!" he shouted. "Ready all ground-to-air defenses!"

"Fire BEFORE you see the whites of their eyes!" the Secretary of Defense screamed at the comm specialist.

The room erupted into a flurry of activity. Colonel Ford barked orders into the telephone. Klaxons and alarms went off, status boards erupted with data as missile warships, aircraft carriers, fleet operation, air force global strike command, and national guard units received orders. Fleet command was issuing urgent orders for warships to steam at flank speed to rallying points. The air force was launching AWACS. NATO command was mobilizing everything it had, France was readying a negotiating team to ensure that invading aliens would not damage any Paris landmarks, Russian warships and submarines immediately started running aground and fouling their anchors as Supreme Command issued conflicting orders. Under cover of a naval communications failure in the British fleet, Argentina landed a Marine assault force on the Falklands (Malvinas!), and every country with so much as a single fighter jet launched the thing in whatever direction they thought the aliens might show up. It was World War Three, with every nation prepped and ready to fire in all directions at once and likely catch each other in the crossfire.

– 5 –

Many major cities around the world again invoked evacuation orders when it became clear the aliens were intent on targeting larger metropolitan areas. Some cities were evacuated quickly because they were prepared for the eventuality. There were some stragglers and stubborn citizens that refused to leave their homes. Most of them would have been forcibly removed were it not for the speed of the alien attack – all emergency responders were recalled and positioned at key locations, mostly to the suburbs to await instructions.

People living in mid-sized and smaller cities were given the option to stay in their homes. Many of those took in their friends and relatives from larger cities. Those without a place to stay were accommodated in libraries, school gymnasiums, and other public spaces. Everyone watched their televisions and news streams on their computers, tablets and smart phones for any updates on the attack. Despite the worldwide panic, most infrastructure was still in working order, however mobile phone service was becoming sporadic due to heavy traffic.

Officials couldn't offer much information, instead advising everyone to stay in their homes or designated areas and rely on their emergency supplies, which most people had stocked up on when it became apparent the approaching object was an alien ship. Some citizens were stoic, facing the unknown with courage, while others were either constantly crying or on the verge of panic.

Cameras turned to the sky above Las Vegas. A swarm of objects were descending out of the clouds towards various buildings. A close-up of one showed a saucer-shaped craft with what looked like a cannon turret on the front.

The ships banked slowly, intermittently firing an orange beam. One beam struck a large hotel, its bright energy temporarily overwhelming the camera and making it difficult for viewers to see detail. They were watching in horror, just as the aliens predicted.

– 6 –

Six hundred kilometers off the California coast Commander "Lynx" Fleigman was sitting in his F-35 Lightning II fighter on the deck of the aircraft carrier Nimitz. He was a 20-year veteran, and would be among the first to fly off the deck to meet the alien threat.

As the deck blast shield rose behind his engine in preparation for launch he was glad to be in the newest, most advanced plane in Navy inventory. His old jet, the F-14, could fly faster and further but the Lightening had the latest stealth technology, weaponry and avionics. The F-35 squadron on Nimitz had only become operational the month before. *The paint job on this plane is barely dry and we're already taking it into combat,* he thought.

At the Catapult Officer's signal Fleigman increased the engine's power to Full. It roared as the plane was restrained by the catapult holdback bar. All instruments checked green so he gave a salute to the Cat Officer and grasped the handles above the instrument panel, keeping his hands free of the controls. The plane lurched forward, pressing him back into the seat. In under three seconds he was airborne and no longer under computer control. He grabbed the control stick and climbed as his wingman launched just seconds behind him.

An EWAC radar aircraft was already airborne and had reported multiple contacts at 250,000 feet, near the top edge of the plane's vertical radar range. "Cap One, bogies are fading in and out, but they appear to be descending fast, 80,000 per minute. ETA three minutes. Be advised radar sketchy. Recommend infrared."

Missiles guided by heat signature were shorter range. *So much for a long range kill,* Fleigman thought, *up close and personal it shall be.* "Roger Flight."

Nimitz was launching one squadron of F-35's and two squadrons of F/A-18's. Both planes had a maximum combat altitude of just over 50,000 feet, so Fleigman would have to wait for the bogie to come to him. He hit the afterburner to gain altitude quicker. Better to engage the enemy high and fast, than low and slow.

Fleigman and his wingman were cruising at 43,000 when the EWAC gave another update.

"Cap One, they're headed right for you, closing subsonic. You should get a visual in a few seconds." He saw it the same time his radar beeped – a metallic saucer-shaped craft with what looked like two gun turrets, one above and one below, near the front of the ship. It wasn't big, maybe the size of his own F-35, but he couldn't get a good radar lock. Like the EWAC officer said, it faded in and out of radar contact, but he could see it clearly.

"You see it Hurly?" Fleigman asked his wingman.

"Yeah Lynx, but can't get a lock. Do you have tone?"

"Negative, no missile tone, we need to get closer."

They didn't have long to wait as the alien craft banked in their direction. Other fighters were simultaneously engaging other alien ships. Fleigman's targeting system gave a lock tone one moment, then lost it an instant later.

"Can't get a lock, but I'm firing anyway. Fox One."

The Sidewinder missile launched, leaving a white plume in its wake as it streaked towards the target. The alien craft moved in a slow s-pattern away from the missile. The Sidewinder corrected, then seemed to loose the target, missing completely, now locking onto the sun and flying skyward.

"Fox Two," Fleigman said as he fired another missile, this time at much closer range – only two kilometers distant. The missile flew true, heading straight to its target.

"You got it Lynx! Splash that bandit!"

The missile flew right into the ship. It emerged from the other side, without detonating.

Neither pilot could speak for a second.

"Hurly, you see that?"

"I thought for sure you hit it. I know you hit it. My turn. Fox One, Fox two!"

Hurly fired two sidewinders. The first went straight through the target without detonating. The second narrowly missed.

"Your first was right on target! This is some kind of advanced defense. Break right," Fleigman ordered. "Let's get around this bandit, approach from the rear."

There was a crackle over the radio, then a strange baritone voice.

"Your crappy missiles are useless against us!"

Fleigman and Hurly flew by the side of the craft.

"Flight," Fleigman reported, "We are passing bogie at 500 meters from its port side. Ident follows."

The top cap of the saucer was darker than the main hull, and was ringed with orange-glowing viewports. There appeared to be a few dents and blast marks, as if the ship had seen better days, and the rounded gun turrets seemed to be tacked on as an afterthought. The lower turret was a lighter color than the top one, which now rotated, following the path of the jets. It fired a stream of bright, orange light, hitting Fleigman's plane, nearly blinding him. The light bounced off the plane in all directions.

"I'm hit!"

After a half-second the alien quit firing as the planes banked out of its field of fire.

"Lynx!" Hurly yelled, sure that his friend was dead.

Fleigman steadied his plane. He saw spots in front of his eyes but the effect quickly subsided so he checked the plane's instrumentation.

"All systems functioning! Hurly, do you see any damage?"

"Negative, you look okay. You were hit dead on, I thought you were finished."

Fleigman looked to his left. An F/A-18 Hornet was hit by a blast from another alien ship, but the Hornet flew on, unharmed.

"What did that voice say, that our missiles were *crappy?*"

– 7 –

The President and his group were anxiously watching the monitors. The screens alternated between maintaining a fix on the mother ships, close-ups of the small alien 'fighters' from Navy ship on-board cameras, and a tactical map of where other alien fighters were being sighted. Lieutenant Gibson held his hand over the phone mouthpiece.

"Commander Phelps, Executive Officer on the Nimitz is giving me an update. There is a fierce battle, with our Navy fighters engaging an equal number of alien fighters. Only there have been no casualties on either side. We have lost no aircraft. And our own weapons are ineffective. Missiles and cannon shells appear to fly right through them."

The President looked to another military advisor, who shrugged his shoulders. The occupants of the room were speechless.

"They may try another weapon type against us that is more effective," said Colonel Ford. We must do the same. Some of our ships have rail guns and acoustic cannons. I'm sure those weapons are being fired as we speak."

An unfamiliar baritone voice came over the loudspeaker, along with the text on the monitor:

Watch as we smash your ships! Cower in fear as we crush your cities!

"No doubt they will adjust their own weapons. We may not have seen their full capabilities yet," said Gibson.

An aide entered the room and handed Colonel Ford a piece of paper. Ford stood up.

"Mr. President, reports are coming in from all over the globe. Thousands of alien fighters are descending on major world cities. A coordinated mass attack is underway," Ford said. "Cities under siege include New York, Las Vegas, Chicago, Toronto, Vancouver, London, Paris, Rome, Moscow, Tokyo—"

"Have our ground forces engaged the enemy?" The President asked.

"Yes sir, fire has been exchanged. We should have a status report in minutes."

– 8 –

Elvis Beckener had been an Elvis impersonator for nearly fifteen years. He had a showman's personality and with the help of voice lessons and hair dye he had some of the King's stage presence, at least enough to send some older female audience members into hysterics when he belted out his rendition of *Love Me Tender.*

Born Shmuel Mordecai Beckener, he changed his name to Elvis at age 32 and was fit enough then to do the King's *"1968 Comeback"* act. As he got older his body changes started to mirror that of the late model *"Moody Blue"* Elvis. That suited him fine, and at 46 he was now the 1976 Elvis, all 260 pounds of him. The puffy, waddling, Jewish Elvis. Mercifully, his stage act no longer included hip gyrations. It was a living.

The first ten days of the alien contact resulted in all the major Las Vegas shows and casinos being shut down, for the first time ever. Then in the last couple of days some shows started up again, including his, when a few tourists started to trickle back into the city.

Now that the alien attack was on, the shows were cancelled again and the city was under evacuation order. Beckener lived where he performed, at the Silverton Vista hotel. The hotel had been evacuated an hour before but Beckener went back to retrieve his prized Harley Davidson belt buckle, which the memorabilia dealer he bought it from years before insisted had been owned by the King himself. The hotel was just inside the restricted perimeter, so Beckener parked well away from the police guarding the major streets and snuck past an unmanned side street barricade.

Inside the restricted zone the streets were deserted. Even the hotel's security personnel had left, locking all the doors behind them. Beckener knew of a loose window in the back kitchen area. He managed to squeeze his bulk through it and get inside. He found the prized belt buckle in his room and put it in his pocket.

He was walking the half-mile back to his car when he heard a peculiar low hum. He looked around and froze. He saw a large saucer-like craft circling around a building, flying slowly towards him. It was the size of a bus, steel-colored, with black streaks on its hull. The fact that it made almost no sound and was flying slowly down the street made it look so utterly weird and terrifying. There was a brief hiss as the ship vented some steam where the top section joined the main hull. The lower gun turret rotated in his direction with a groaning metal-on-metal sound. He felt the hair on the back of his neck stand on end. He couldn't move.

Beckener was at the intersection of a major street, and the thing was coming at him from a side street. He could either stick to the side street to try and make it back to his car, or run the shorter distance along the main street to a manned barricade, two hundred yards away. Police and firemen at the barricade saw the alien craft and were shouting and waving at him.

After a second Beckener's flight response took over. He ran towards the barricade as fast as his 260 pounds of out-of-shape bulk and questionable knees would let him.

– 9 –

Bill Fornello was a member of the Las Vegas Fire Department stationed at one of the many barricades in the city. Suburban fire stations were still operating normally but those within the perimeter had been closed, their members assigned to crowd control at shopping malls or at barricades like this one, which in addition to himself had a police officer, a city sewage inspector, and a news reporter. It was Bill's job to keep citizens out of the Las Vegas Strip, behind the waist-high movable steel fence. It hadn't been difficult so far, as most citizens wanted to be as far as possible from what was deemed a probable target for attack.

An hour earlier they had seen three Merlins spiral down from the sky and disappear among the buildings downtown. Somebody in the news had remarked that with their steel-like exterior and orange beam spewing gun barrels, the alien scout ships (or fighters, or whatever they were) looked like something conjured up by a deranged magician, and so the name Merlin stuck.

The four barricade members had been eating sandwiches delivered by volunteers when the sewage inspector started yelling and pointing, "Look! One of those things is chasing Elvis! C'mon Elvis, get over here. Run! You can make it!"

Fornello dropped his half-eaten sandwich and looked down the street. He saw the edge of a Merlin emerge from around a corner, chasing a huge Elvis dressed in a billowy, sequined white suit lumbering towards them. The news reporter launched a small battery operated hovering camera controlled by his mobile phone towards the Merlin.

The rest of the group clutched the fence and yelled encouragement. Elvis was about fifty yards from the barricade when a deep, menacing voice boomed from the alien ship:

"Observe as we destroy your cultural leaders! Watch in horror, then know we will come for you next!"

The Merlin unleashed a blast of orange beam from its lower gun barrel, hitting Elvis full-on. He fell into a heap, shuddering violently as the beam bounced off of him and the surrounding pavement.

"They killed him! Damn you bastards!" shouted the policeman, shaking his fist at the Merlin. "You killed Elvis, you sons of bitches!"

The Merlin stopped firing as the cameraman's small hovercraft flew past it. The Merlin slowly turned to follow the hovercraft, firing on it. The hovercraft spiraled down and crashed onto the street. The Merlin continued away from the barricade, back downtown.

Fornello opened the barricade. "Come on," he ordered, "Let's retrieve the body before that thing notices us."

He and the police officer ran over to Beckener, who groaned.

"He's still alive!" said Fornello. "Let's get him back."

They supported Beckener stumbling and limping as fast as they could back to the barricade. They sat him down on a crate.

"Whole lotta shakin' goin' on," said Beckener, who appeared dazed.

"Elvis! Elvis, you okay?" Fornello asked. Fat Elvis nodded his head slowly. Several sequins came off his cape and fell on the pavement.

"Yeah, I think so. Man, that hurt!" he said, picking up the broken sequins.

The barricade crew looked at each other in surprise.

"How can this be? That Merlin hit him full force. You saw him go down," said the police officer.

"How do you feel?" Fornello asked. Beckener was regaining his senses.

"Like I was hit by a hundred bee stings."

"Bee stings? That's it?"

"You ever been stung by a bee, man? It hurts! And I felt like I was stung by a hundred of 'em!"

"How are you now? Any pain?"

Beckener stood up and reached into his right pants pocket.

"Nope. Feel fine. I have to get to my car. Thanks for your help guys!"

Beckener handed each of them a ticket to his show, and walked off to find his car. The others were speechless as they watched him go. Elvis had left the barricade.

– 10 –

Sergeant "Thrasher" Blake was commanding his M1A2 Abrams main battle tank on the Las Vegas strip. The crew was pursuing a Merlin spotted zigzagging in and out of the side streets along the strip. The tank was fast on pavement, capable of hitting speeds of up to 40 mph but the need to avoid abandoned vehicles on the road was drastically slowing them down. They saw smoke in the distance. Word was that a Merlin had taken out a car dealership.

Thrasher wanted to be the first tank commander to bag a Merlin. Another tank crew had fired on a Merlin but missed. *How do you miss such a big target,* Thrasher thought. The M1's targeting system was state of the art, and when not falling out of the sky the ships looked like they were slow moving, even cumbersome when low to the ground. Maybe the other crew got nervous and fired on override. Thrasher's crew wouldn't make that mistake.

He was observing ahead through the viewfinder when he saw it, a slow-moving, steel-colored saucer, with twin menacing gun turrets.

"Contact! Three blocks ahead, Merlin closing. Prepare to fire M830."

The Loader chose the round and loaded the main gun. "Ready to fire," he said.

The Merlin was flying slowly directly towards them, about 500 meters away, well within the effective range of the main gun.

"Fire when ready," Thrasher instructed the gunner.

The tank rocked back slightly as the massive 120mm

gun fired. Much of the noise was muffled by the communication headphones each crewmember wore, but they could feel the concussive force in their chests. Thrasher had been in the M1 for seven years and was still impressed by the gun's power.

Thrasher kept his eye on the Merlin as the gun fired. The expected explosion on the target did not come. Instead, a second later there was an explosion about a kilometer down the street in a hotel.

"Gunner, you missed! Reload!"

Again the tank thundered as the gun fired. Again the round was ineffective against the target, hitting the same hotel down the street.

"Gunner, what the hell happened? Is your targeting system malfunctioning?"

"Negative Sarge, we were dead on! I can't explain it."

Now the Merlin was bearing down on them. A booming voice could be heard over the intercom.

"You will suffer greatly for your attack. Prepare to be obliterated!"

Thrasher knew their first shells were ineffective. He needed to change strategy.

"Get us out of here. Take us east down the next side street. Reload with a 1028 and prepare to fire."

The Merlin fired before the tank could start its turn down the street. There was a bright light through the tank's periscope and the crew could hear what sounded like hail hitting the armor plate.

"We're taking fire!" said the driver.

"Keep moving! Take us out of its line of sight," said Thrasher.

The tank made it down the side street at high speed, away from the Merlin.

Thrasher's instrument panel showed green. "Status report. You guys see any damage?"

"Negative Sarge, no damage," each crew member reported.

Just then some encrypted orders came over the com. Thrasher couldn't believe his eyes, but there it was: an order to retreat.

"We're to break off attack. Fall back to base."

– 11 –

The peculiar battles raged for hours in some cities. It began to dawn on the military strategists, commanders, troops and civilians that all the damage being done to buildings and property was entirely from friendly fire, not from the aliens, whose weapons seemed to be completely ineffectual. Tanks and aircraft fired at Merlins, always with the same result: shells went through the target, sometimes hitting important structures behind. Merlins fired at tanks, aircraft and people, with no ill effects.

The order came through that alien craft were only to be fired upon if no buildings or strategically important areas were immediately behind the target. The call went out for other weapon types, such as flame throwers, acoustic cannons, and electromagnetic pulse generators. In each case there was no visible damage done to the Merlins.

After two days it was obvious the armed forces needed to be scaled back. They were doing far more damage to metropolitan areas than the aliens were. A ceasefire order was initiated while the President and his advisory team at the Pentagon assessed the situation. Dr. Himmler cleared his throat and stood up to deliver his report.

"Mizderr Brezident, I beeleef zat ze aliens are vrum anozer temporal plane." Himmler was staring imperiously at a point on the far wall. "Normally zis vood zugjest zey vood be kombleetly undetectable und invisible to us and to zem. But due to an as yet uneggs-plained venomenon, eezer naturally occurrink or by artifice, zis dimensional shift haz allowed zis door to open halfway, zo to speak."

Nobody spoke for a moment. The President leaned to his aide and whispered, "I can't understand him."

The aide looked over at Gibson. The lieutenant nodded and went downstairs.

"This door, can it be closed, shutting the aliens out from us?" Colonel Ford asked.

"I do not beeleef zo," Himmler replied. Whereffer ze venomena is rezbonsiple, it is beyond our means to invluenz it."

Just then Gibson returned, and nodded to the President and his aide. There was a crackle over the intercom.

"Uh, this is chief engineer Jones from the pit. We could really use Dr. Himmler down here. Doctor Himmler, would you come down to the workstation area and join the engineers? Uh, immediately?"

Himmler looked exasperated. "I really don't zink I should—"

"Please Doctor," the President interjected. "The engineers could really use your help."

Gibson moved over to Himmler and gently tugged on his elbow. Himmler got up and dejectedly walked downstairs with Gibson.

Major Scott reached over to Himmler's binder.

"I can fill in for Dr. Himmler, sir."

"Yes, thank god for that," said the President. "I mean… go ahead, Major. What's the bottom line?"

"We can see and communicate with the aliens, but we cannot interact with them physically. Our plane of existence is slightly off from theirs, almost as if we are occupying the same space but at a slightly different time."

"Then why are we able to see and hear them?" Ford asked quickly.

"Ve are unsure as to ze reazon for zis," Himmler's voice came through the intercom. "Ve are zdill analyzink ze zituazhun. Ze best example I can gif is a zlight time variation zat somehow allows limited interaction between dimensions. But zey cannot harm us."

Himmler was looking up forlornly to the conference room from the workstation area.

The President gestured wildly in the direction of the intercom. "Mute that thing," he whispered harshly. His aide hit the Mute button.

"Major Scott?" asked the President. "Why can we see and hear them?"

"We aren't completely sure," replied Scott. "We're still analyzing the situation. The best example I can give is a slight time variation that somehow allows limited interaction between universes. But they can't harm us."

"Zat is vut I just said," came Himmler's voice from the intercom.

The aide tapped the Mute button repeatedly. It didn't appear to be working. He shrugged his shoulders, his eyes darting around the room. The President scowled.

"Neither can we harm them," said Ford. "This doesn't mean they won't eventually find an effective weapon."

"All ze more reazon vor uz to negotiate," said Himmler.

"Thank you doctor," said the President, while closing his eyes tightly and holding the bridge of his nose. He appeared to suffering from a headache.

– 12 –

There were multiple attempts by several governments and the UN to negotiate with the aliens, who seldom replied except to insult the governments and people of Earth. In the Control Room the following messages were received:

Your attempts to appease us are laughable. We will crush you like bugs!

We will kidnap the most attractive, middle-aged members of your race, otherwise known to you as MILFs, and have our way with them! You can keep the US President's wife, we don't find her attractive at all.

The President was outraged. His face turned red, then purple. He swept some binders off the table and stood up, shouting.

"How dare they! Lousy scumbags! Who do they think they are? We should insult them back! They wouldn't know an attractive woman from a fire hydrant! Tell them what Jerks they are! Jerks from space!"

One of his aides tried to calm him down.

"This is what they want sir, for us to lose control. We should ignore them. You've been under a lot of stress."

"You think it's easy running the country and taking care of the needs of a younger woman? Well it's not!"

"Sir, please!" The aide implored.

The President stood there, breathing heavily. He tried to regain his composure.

"Yes, right, composure. I'm composed. As annoying as they are, the aliens don't seem to pose any real danger. As much as it pains me to say it, we've got to ignore their taunts."

The President adjusted his tie and sat down.

"What is our current status?"

The aide turned his attention to the computer tablet in front of him. On the display was a graph showing the country's GDP performance over the past month.

"We need to get our economy back on track. We can't keep the military at maximum readiness much longer. We'll bankrupt ourselves. In view of the diminished danger posed by the aliens, all armed forces are to go from Defcon 3 to Defcon 4, as per your order. All major cities require road, building, and infrastructure repair, due to damage done by our own forces. Limited numbers of workers will be allowed back into the cities for repair and utility maintenance. Small armed units will remain in cities with a heavy alien presence. We suggest letting people back into their homes in stages."

– 13 –

Gradually the public's terror subsided and turned to puzzlement as it was revealed the alien's weapons were ineffective. What were the aliens doing here? What were the motives behind their so-called attacks? Weeks after the first landing the aliens pressed on blaring their insults.

"We have annihilated mightier civilizations than yours.
Kneel before us or we will obliterate you!"

As people returned to their homes some challenged the Merlins directly. They would stand in the street shielding themselves with garbage can lids, shouting their own insults. Often the Merlins would turn on them, unleashing as a blast of orange beam.

"Impudent human scum! Feel the wrath of your
overlords!"

As long as people carried some sort of shield, pain was minimized. A few tough guys stood in the street shirtless, betting each other who could remain standing longest in the face of a Merlin onslaught. Most people collapsed or ran after five or ten seconds, but some of the more stubborn (usually drunk) ones endured a minute or more of "Merlin Fire." The Merlin then gave up and moved on, all the while booming more insults.

"You are fools! We toy with you at our leisure!"

Back in the Control Room the President, Colonel Ford, Lieutenant Gibson, Major Scott, Dr. Himmler and various advisors were sitting around the conference table watching a news report on the large monitor. Three Merlins had ganged up on a house, each of them blasting the roof, concentrating their fire on a single spot. The owner was in the yard throwing garden tools at the Merlins, the tools passing through the ships harmlessly.

After a few seconds there was a puff of smoke as a piece of shingle blew off.

"Assholes!" the man screamed, shaking his fist in the air. "Go bother someone else, you dickheads!"

The Merlins disengaged, leaving the owner running for his garden hose to douse the smoldering shingle, which probably would have extinguished itself anyway. The characteristic Merlin taunt accompanied their leaving:

"Let this be an example to all disobedient humans!"

The President gestured back at the monitor and nodded to an aide, who turned it off.

"That is the problem gentlemen. They're everywhere, and they're tormenting common citizens. It's relentless. People are complaining bitterly. Recommendations. I want recommendations!"

Dr. Himmler stood up and spoke after casting a condescending look at everyone.

"Ve are not in dane-cher of beeink zubchuck-ated or conquered by a superior raze. Clearly Mr. President, zey haf advanced technology, but it cannot be used against uz and neezer can ve appropriate it for our own uze. All attempts to enter into a meanink-vool dialog wiz zem haf vailt. Zey can understand uz, but zey invariably choose to brush off our attampts at peace, preferrink to lob more inzults und threats. Zey appear to be psychotic, or perhaps neurotic."

There was silence for a moment. The President turned to Major Scott.

"Major, what are your thoughts?"

"We're not in danger of being conquered by these aliens. Clearly, they have advanced technology, but it can't be used against us. They can understand us, but they invariably choose to brush off our attempts at peace, preferring to lob insults and threats. They appear to be psychotic, or at least neurotic."

"I see," nodded the President.

Himmler waved his hands theatrically and huffed as he sat down, fuming.

The President leaned over to his aide. "What's he doing back up here?" he whispered.

"Sorry sir, he must have snuck in as the door was closing. Won't happen again."

"Well, things can't go on like this," colonel Ford piped up. "Tens of millions of citizens are stressed. They can't sleep. The bloody Merlins fly up and down residential streets at all hours, booming moronic insults. Absenteeism in the armed forces is way up. Nobody can get anything done."

Himmler pushed his notebook in front of Major Scott and slammed his finger down on a specific paragraph.

Scott glanced at it then addressed the President.

"Mr. President, if something is not done to combat this terrorism, productivity in the population will decrease to the point of recession. Action must be taken."

"Yes, good thinking. Thank you Major," said the President. Dr. Himmler huffed and rolled his eyes.

The President thought for a moment. He exchanged a few words with his aide and turned his attention back to the conference table.

"We need to come up with an advertising campaign. It should make fun of the aliens, and mention how impotent they are. Make it funny, and have kids laughing and pointing at them. Send the message out that the best way to deal with the aliens is to ignore them."

– 14 –

Products were showing up that claimed to be "Merlin proof." A television commercial showed a young man walking arm-in-arm with his smiling girlfriend. When a Merlin appeared, the woman looked frightened, but the man opened an umbrella, which handily deflected the orange beam. The couple laughed as they continued walking, a voiceover saying *"Don't let the space jerks ruin your day! The new Merlin-proof umbrella deflects the painful Merlin ray every time!"*

Another television spot showed kids playing in a park wearing what looked like transparent raincoats over their regular clothes, complete with hats. A Merlin swooped overhead, blasting the children, who continued playing without taking notice. The commercial cut to a mother who smiled and said, *"Thanks* Merlin-proof! *Now I don't need to worry when my kids go out on heavy Merlin days! Available in a variety of trim colors, so your child is always fashionable."*

– 15 –

Three months after the landing, strategic meetings reverted to weekly in a more comfortable conference room at the Pentagon. Major Scott was giving his weekly status report to the President.

"Mr. President, I want to address reports that the invaders have been using social media. Most Facebook pages that have shown up claiming to be from the aliens are hoaxes, but a few appear to be genuine. They contain highly accurate information on mother ship orbital positions that only we, and the aliens, know."

"Und do not forget ze Twitter postings," said Himmler through the intercom.

"Yes! Yes! Thank you Doctor!" the President replied, then gestured to his aide, who quickly hit the mute button.

The aide blushed. "Sorry sir," he said. The President turned back to the table.

"I've seen those pages. They are full of brags and insults about how superior they are to us."

Lieutenant Gibson called up an alien Facebook page. It contained an overhead, Merlin-perspective photo of a cowering Vice President being blasted while running to his limousine. The caption read, *Check back often for updates on how we plan to destroy your leaders!*

"Yes sir," Gibson said. "But what's interesting is a report from a young girl who claims to have had a private Twitter dialog with an alien. Over time the girl and individual alien have developed a friendship, and the alien has apologized for his people's behavior. He claims that they belong to a regime similar to that of North Korea, where the people have to live with fanatical patriotism and a daily onslaught of boasting and ranting. For centuries they have been ruled by an arrogant dictator who demands blind obedience. Most of them are indeed fanatics, although a few, like this individual, seem more reasonable, but have no choice but to play along and follow their leader's orders."

"Is there a way we could use that to our advantage? Can we turn some of them?"

"Doubtful sir. They have been indoctrinated so long they will likely continue following the same path. They came here to conquer us, and realized almost immediately it was impossible due to the temporal phase difference. Nevertheless, they wish to save face and continue their useless attempts to instill terror rather than suffer an embarrassing retreat."

"So we're stuck with these pests? Have we made any progress in finding a way to get rid of them?"

"I regret to report the science teams are no closer to uncovering the nature of the Merlin's technology, the orange beam, or what can be done to rid the earth of them."

The President looked to Colonel Ford.

"Same report from the armed forces sir. We have tried new weapons such as high-powered lasers and particle beams, sound cannons, water cannons, confetti launchers to confuse their sensors, teams of professional insulters using megaphones, but nothing affects the Merlins."

Just then the President's BlackBerry vibrated on the table. He picked it up and opened the message:

"You will not win a second term! We have been exchanging hot messages with your Mother-in-law. She will share a hotel domicile with us!"

A vein in the President's neck bulged as he read the text.

"Those bastards have tapped into my BlackBerry!"

"Yes, it took a little longer for the BlackBerries to be compromised," said Gibson. "The aliens hacked into iOS and Android last Tuesday. They're sending threats and insults to prominent government personnel, and even some ordinary citizens. What's worse is they sometimes misdirect any replies you make to random contacts in your address book."

"What about Windows Phone?" asked one of the President's aides.

"They haven't bothered with Windows Phone. Not enough market penetration to make it worthwhile."

The President typed furiously and then hit Send. An instant later Himmler, who was back in the lower Control Room, felt his phone vibrate. The Doctor was aghast at what he read. His voice shook with indignation over the intercom.

"Mr. President. I am sorry you feel zat vay about me und my ancestors."

The President sighed and rubbed his temples.

"Sorry Doctor. Wrong number."

"He can't hear you sir, the intercom is on Mute."

"Oh, can you... oh, never mind. What does the economic report look like?"

"Quite good actually, sir. People are back to work, and as we've seen, new Merlin-resistant industries have opened up, with noise-cancelling panels in homes to cut down on the sound volume of Merlin insults, suit jackets, hats and sunglasses that are 'orange ray proof,' and new vacation spots appearing in Merlin-free areas."

"Well that's something at least."

"Still, divorce rates and prescription drug use have gone up. Some people are driven nearly insane by the constant taunting."

"I know what that feels like," said the President. "A damn Merlin hovered outside my bedroom window last night, making inappropriate remarks about the First Lady's mother. I tell you, I can't take much more of this. By the way, what does MILF mean?"

"Perhaps we can install those noise-cancelling sound panels in your bedroom sir."

– 16 –

Six months later Colonel Ford chaired the latest meeting, which had reverted to every two weeks. Aside from the President, the regular members were in attendance, except for Himmler, who had resigned and returned to Germany.

"Gentlemen, due to some urgent personal issues, the President will not be joining us today. You have no doubt read about it in the news already, but the President and the First Lady have separated. Chalk that one up to the Merlins. They taunted the First Family mercilessly, even following them to their vacation home. Additionally, this will be my last meeting. I'm due for retirement this year, and since the aliens are clearly not a threat, I have decided to take retirement now. I'll be a consultant to the private sector on developing new Merlin-resistant products."

"Congratulations sir," said Lieutenant Gibson.

"Major Scott, your report please."

Scott stood and retrieved the room monitor's remote control.

"Most areas of society have learned to adapt with the presence of the aliens. Children have been reassured the Merlins are all trash talk and can't hurt them. Industry and education are now largely unaffected. People are learning to cope, and divorce rates have stabilized, almost returning to pre-Merlin levels. We even have some good news – international conflicts have gone down by 20% as nations have cooperated in innovating new Merlin-proof strategies and products for the public. However, there are two main groups that have been adversely affected by the Merlins."

Scott activated the monitor. The scene showed a riot in progress.

"The aliens are very adept at observing where their taunts are most effective. The two groups that have had trouble adapting are professional golfers and the extremely religious."

The scene cut to show a golf course where players were hurling their clubs at the Merlins, while the ships hovered and blasted the green. The Merlin voice could be heard blaring away.

> *"Your game is for childish baby men!*
> *You are unskilled fools!"*

"Merlins congregate at golf tournaments. They wait for an important shot, then emerge from behind the trees with their taunts and screw up the game. They have also been observed ganging up to blast the ball closest to the cup, sometimes setting it on fire. One tournament leader had to be restrained as he ran from caddy to caddy, heaving as many clubs as he could at the Merlins. I understand he has been taken in for psychological evaluation, and may never golf again."

"Poor bastard," said Ford. "You also said something about the effect on churches?"

"Yes. The average churchgoer takes things in stride, believing their character is being tested, and so they cope with the insults to their religion in quiet dignity. However, the more devout, or fanatical churchgoers, of every faith, have taken great offence and are becoming irrational. Observe."

The scene cut to show a church parking lot where pitchfork and shotgun wielding churchgoers seemed to be in a standoff with a Merlin. Scott turned up the volume. Over the shouts of people could be heard the booming alien voice:

"Your prayers are misplaced! You will worship us, your masters! Kneel before us, or suffer our wrath!"

Colonel Ford sighed.

"Don't those people know that their reactions only encourage the Merlins? They should be ignoring them."

"Yes sir," Said Scott. "But religious fanatics, like golfers, react differently than the average person. They are beyond reason. Irrational savages, really."

Everybody nodded in agreement. Colonel Ford placed his appointment book in his briefcase, signifying the meeting was over. They shook hands with Colonel Ford and wished him luck.

On the way to his car the colonel could hear that familiar low hum, so he unfurled his umbrella (they had become an essential accessory for everyone, no matter the weather). Gibson watched from the conference room window as the Merlin came out of nowhere, blasting away at his former commanding officer, its orange beam deflected by the colonel's umbrella. The ever-dignified Colonel Ford paid it little notice as he got into his car and drove off to retirement.

– Epilogue –

Forty years later, Gibson, who had long since been promoted to full Colonel, was going over his final report on the aliens. Like his old mentor Colonel Ford, Gibson was a career military man, devoting his life to his country. Now on his day of retirement he reflected on the Merlin nuisance.

As the years went on, the number of invading Merlin ships gradually dwindled from tens of thousands, to thousands, to hundreds as most of them defected from their bizarre mission, returning to an orbiting mother ship. Now only one mother ship remained in earth orbit, the other four having presumably left for their home world or another planet to harass.

A year ago there were only an estimated twelve Merlins remaining on earth, a handful each in North America and Europe, one in Australia and one in South America. The woman that had developed an on-line friendship with one of the few reasonable aliens had passed on a final message that the remaining Merlins were those of the Great Leader himself and his loyal caucus. Everyone else had taken off.

After decades of the media ignoring the Merlins, now that they were so rare, an appearance by a one was a big event. At any reported sighting news crews or remote-controlled drone cameras were dispatched to meet it. Crowds gathered to watch the show as the Merlin invariably fired on the news team or camera.

The crowed cheered as the Merlin boomed one of its usual taunts:

"Human fools! Cower in fear as we destroy your primitive civilization and force you to do our bidding!"

In forty years, the aliens had not revealed their physical appearance, nor volunteered any information about their home world, despite many requests that they do so. As he signed the report, Gibson realized something surprising. Two generations had grown up not having known anything of a world without Merlins. For over half the living population of earth, the aliens had always been present, first as a threat, then an irritation, then finally as a curiosity.

Last month there were only two verified Merlins left on earth. As Gibson was about to file the report, his administrative assistant rushed into his office with information that the two ships were facing off on Constitution Avenue, near the White House. It was the first time this year that any Merlins had been seen in the United States. Gibson and his assistant raced in his car to the scene. A crowd was beginning to gather on the sidewalks, along with numerous armed White House security personnel.

At first the ships hovered silently, facing each other, separated by about a hundred meters. The tense silence was punctuated when each occasionally vented steam. Then they began taunting each other.

*"You are weak! You are incapable of ruling this world.
I am Supreme Ruler of Earth!"*

*"No, it is you who are weak! I rule this world with an
iron fist! Leave or be destroyed!"*

After a few more threats were traded the Merlins fired on one another. Each ship glowed red hot as they exchanged fire. After a moment the Merlins simultaneously exploded, disintegrating in a flash, leaving no traces.

The colonel felt a light tap from the phone chip in his left outer ear canal, indicating an incoming call. He winked his left eye to answer the call. It was the chief engineer from the control center.

"Sir, the last mother ship is leaving orbit. They've left a final message."

"Let's hear it," Gibson replied.

"They say, *We are not the only race in the galaxy that says you are insolent fools. Punk you later.*"

Acknowledgements

Edited by Howard Carson
hcarson@gmail.com

Core ship design used under licence from turbosquid.com

Ship digital enhancements by Peter Macchione
petermacc@hotmail.com
www.petermacchione.com

Background image courtesy of NASA

Thanks to Greta for her valued support

We Have Seen The Enemy and They Are Odd
ISBN 978-0-9868364-7-3

Also by Sunbow Press

From Shy To Social:
The Shy Man's Guide To Personal & Dating Success

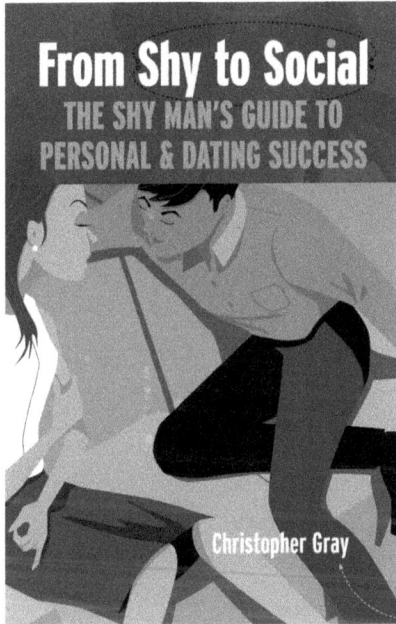

"Engaging, well-researched and frequently hilarious, *From Shy To Social* is one of those rare self-help books that feels like you're being coached and encouraged by a trusted friend. An absolute must-read for all of the love shy men out there."
  – Sofi Papamarko, Relationship Columnist & Contributor to
        The Huffington Post and *The Globe & Mail*

"This is an important topic that affects so many men, who will be happy to have this book!"
        – Liza Fromer, host of *The Morning Show*, Global TV